Original title:
Crystal Nights

Copyright © 2024 Swan Charm
All rights reserved.

Author: Paulina Pähkel
ISBN HARDBACK: 978-9916-79-915-4
ISBN PAPERBACK: 978-9916-79-916-1
ISBN EBOOK: 978-9916-79-917-8

Mystery in the Gleaming Dark

In shadows deep, where whispers dwell,
A secret tale begins to swell.
The stars above, they twinkle bright,
Guarding dreams in the quiet night.

Through twisted paths, the echoes call,
A haunting song, a silken thrall.
Beneath the moon's soft silver glow,
Mysteries hide, and feelings flow.

The rustling leaves, a lover's sigh,
As ghosts of time begin to fly.
Each step we take, a heartbeat near,
Reflecting hopes, dissolving fear.

In every corner, shadows dance,
A fleeting glimpse, a whispered chance.
The night, a cloak, so snug and tight,
Embraces dreams that spark the light.

So wander forth in gleaming dark,
Let curiosity leave its mark.
In every twist, in every turn,
Find the light for which you yearn.

Veils of Light

In the dawn's gentle grace,
Veils of light softly trace.
Whispers of dreams take flight,
Painting the world so bright.

Clouds drift like silent ships,
With sun's warm, golden tips.
Every shadow fades fast,
As day awakens at last.

Mountains blush in warm hue,
Beneath skies so vast and blue.
Hope dances with delight,
In each pulse of shining light.

Leaves sway with a soft tune,
Kissed by the sun and moon.
Nature sings with pure bliss,
A moment we can't miss.

The Silent Sparkle

In a world cloaked in shade,
Silent sparkles cascade.
Stars linger in soft nights,
Whispering secret lights.

Moonbeams weave through the trees,
Carried softly by the breeze.
Each twinkle holds a story,
Wrapped in peace and glory.

Stillness draws hearts to meet,
In rhythms calm and sweet.
Every glance blooms anew,
As darkness fades to blue.

The heart beats out a prayer,
In the stillness that we share.
Each sparkle a gentle kiss,
Time woven into bliss.

Frost-Kissed Fantasies

Frost-kissed dreams arise,
Underneath the winter skies.
Crystal whispers in the air,
Painting each branch with care.

Fields draped in silver light,
Glisten softly in the night.
Nature wears its frosty crown,
A sparkling, glittering gown.

Every footstep leaves a trace,
In this still, enchanted place.
Hushed breaths waltz with the freeze,
In the grip of winter's ease.

Snowflakes dance, spin, and twirl,
In the silence they unfurl.
A canvas pure and white,
Holds our deepest dreams tonight.

Ambers in the Night

Flames flicker, shadows play,
In the embers of the day.
Hearts glow with warm delight,
As we gather through the night.

Stories shared, laughter bright,
Underneath the starry light.
Each moment feels so right,
In the embrace of the night.

Whispers drift on the breeze,
Carried softly through the trees.
In the glow, we ignite,
All our dreams, pure and bright.

As the moon begins to rise,
Hope reflects in our eyes.
In the warmth, we unite,
With ambers burning bright.

Fragments of Starlight

In the night sky's embrace,
Twinkling gems do race,
Stories lost in time,
Echoes of a rhyme.

Fall of light so bright,
Guiding dreams in flight,
Each a timeless spark,
Whispering in the dark.

Glimmers on the sea,
Dancing wild and free,
Carried on the breeze,
With such graceful ease.

Woven through our fate,
Threads of love and hate,
Fragments here remain,
Even through the pain.

Hopes that gently shine,
In this heart of mine,
Count the stars with care,
Find the light up there.

Reflections in the Mist

Upon the silent lake,
Where shadows gently wake,
Whispers float on air,
Secrets soft and rare.

Veils of gray embrace,
Nature's calm, soft grace,
Mirrors of the soul,
As we seek the whole.

Glimpses of the past,
Memories that last,
Fleeting, like a breath,
Waking life from death.

Quiet shimmers rise,
Beneath the dusky skies,
In the world we find,
Reflections intertwined.

Veiled in morning light,
Lost within the sight,
Every drop a sign,
In this space divine.

Whispering Frost

On the edge of dawn,
Nature's breath is drawn,
Crystals form with grace,
Magic takes its place.

Chill caresses skin,
Where the dreams begin,
Footsteps soft and slow,
In the morning glow.

Frozen tales do weave,
In the webs we leave,
Sculpted by the night,
In a world so bright.

Hushed beneath the trees,
Feeling winter's tease,
Whispers in the breeze,
Filling hearts with ease.

Every breath a song,
Deep as winter's throng,
Carried far and wide,
With the world as guide.

Shimmering Veils

A dance of colors bright,
In the fading light,
Veils of dreams unfurled,
Painting of the world.

Softly shadows sway,
As night steals the day,
Mysteries concealed,
In the heart revealed.

Through the layers cast,
Echoes of the past,
Floating in the air,
Wishes lost in prayer.

Twilight gently glows,
Where the river flows,
Rippling with desire,
Setting hearts afire.

Every thread we trace,
Finds a warm embrace,
In this soft relief,
Shimmering belief.

Fragments of the Moonlight

Soft whispers in the night,
Lost dreams take to flight,
Gentle beams on the sea,
A dance wild and free.

Shadows blend with the glow,
Where secrets ebb and flow,
Silvery trails adorn
The edges of the morn.

In the hush of the dark,
A fleeting, tender spark,
Fragments begin to weave,
Stories that we believe.

Beneath the skies so vast,
Echoes of the past,
Illuminate our fears,
Transforming silent tears.

The moonlight's soft embrace,
A sanctuary of grace,
In every quiet sigh,
We find the reasons why.

Whispering Frost

Chill winds caress the trees,
A breath of winter's ease,
Delicate flakes descend,
Nature's quiet friend.

Morning dew on the ground,
A sparkling, crystal crown,
Whispers of cold delight,
In the soft pale light.

Silhouettes, sharp and bright,
Enhance the tranquil sight,
While layers wrap the earth,
Embracing hidden birth.

Frost-kissed meadows wide,
Where shadowed secrets hide,
Each flake a fleeting grace,
A moment to embrace.

Underneath the still sky,
Time slows and we comply,
In frost, the world transforms,
In silence, beauty warms.

Luminous Veils

In twilight's soft embrace,
Veils of light interlace,
Colors dance and merge,
A vibrant, growing surge.

Shimmering hues unfold,
Stories yet untold,
Layers of light cascade,
Magic never fades.

Above, the heavens wink,
While stars begin to blink,
Guiding hearts to roam,
In the vast unknown.

Silken threads entwined,
Mysteries designed,
In the glow we find,
A path that's well defined.

With every breath we take,
A luminous awake,
Carried by the light,
Chasing dreams through the night.

Echoes of Starlight

Whispers of the night sky,
Softly, they come by,
Echoes drift and sing,
A cosmic offering.

Stars, they blink and sway,
Guiding hearts that stray,
In the stillness, grace,
A warm, celestial place.

Fleeting moments shared,
In silence, hearts bared,
Each twinkle a reply,
As we watch and sigh.

Through galaxies we roam,
Finding pieces of home,
Bright trails of the past,
An energy steadfast.

In the tapestry bright,
We've woven our flight,
As echoes of starlight,
Carry us into night.

Glimmering Horizons

The sun kisses the sea,
Waves dance with delight,
Colors bleed in the sky,
A canvas ignites.

Distant mountains stand tall,
Guardians of the night,
Where dreams softly call,
And hearts take flight.

Each star winks from above,
A secret to behold,
Whispers of lost love,
In stories left untold.

Time holds its sweet breath,
Moments intertwined,
In the hush of twilight,
We're forever aligned.

So let the night guide,
With a gentle embrace,
Glimmering horizons,
In timeless space.

Whispers of Refracted Light

Morning breaks so clear,
Sunbeams pierce the fog,
Nature starts to stir,
As life's quiet song.

Through leaves, sunlight plays,
A dance of shadows cast,
In this fleeting phase,
We dream of the past.

Colors merge and weave,
In a radiant stream,
Each hue, a reprieve,
From a waking dream.

Listen to the glow,
It carries tales anew,
Of places we may go,
And skies of brilliant hue.

Whispers soft and low,
In the warmth of the day,
Refracted light will show,
The magic on our way.

Luminous Memories

In the heart of the night,
Stars twinkle like gems,
Each one a beacon bright,
Of where our love stems.

Moments wrapped in light,
Flickering like flames,
Together in this flight,
We cherish the same.

Time flows like a stream,
Carrying our dreams,
Echoes of laughter gleam,
In moonlight beams.

Every shadow holds fast,
A story to be told,
Of the lives we've amassed,
And the love we uphold.

Hold on tight, dear friend,
To these luminous days,
In our hearts, they blend,
In eternal ways.

Boundless Skies Above

Clouds drift soft and slow,
A canvas vast and wide,
Where dreams are free to grow,
In the blue of the tide.

Every gust of wind,
Carries whispers of hope,
As horizons extend,
And we learn to cope.

Time floats like a bird,
Gliding through the air,
In silent, sweet accord,
With the world we share.

Look up, and you'll find,
The stars start to sing,
A symphony for minds,
In flight, on the wing.

Under boundless skies,
Our spirits intertwine,
With every sunrise,
A love that's divine.

Dazzling Silhouettes

In twilight's embrace, shadows dance,
Figures arise, caught in a trance.
Whispers of night in the cool air,
Dreams intertwine, woven with care.

Stars peek through, a velvet sigh,
Guiding the lost, as they wander by.
Moonlit paths, secrets unfold,
Stories of old in the silence told.

Silhouettes glow in the fading light,
Captured moments, both fragile and bright.
Eclipsed by time, yet ever near,
Echoes of laughter, crystalline clear.

Colors blend where the day meets the night,
A stunning canvas, a glorious sight.
Each fleeting shadow, a tale of the day,
Crafting the magic, as they fade away.

Beneath the stars, a promise flies,
In dazzling form, beneath endless skies.
Echoing dreams in the night's caress,
Silhouettes gleam in their soft finesse.

Shimmering Afterglow

Radiant hues paint the sky,
As day bows down, the sun says goodbye.
Twilight drapes the world in gold,
In this moment, a story unfolds.

Ripples of light on the water's face,
Reflecting memories, time can't erase.
Gentle whispers of a fading day,
Linger like dreams that steal away.

The horizon glows, a soft embrace,
Fading echoes in this sacred space.
Every heartbeat, the world slows down,
As stars awaken, a shimmering crown.

Colors entwine in a peaceful blend,
Each fleeting second, a treasure to spend.
The afterglow dances on the lake,
A serene moment, for beauty's sake.

In the twilight, all worries cease,
The shimmering whispers bring the heart peace.
As night falls gently, spirits lift high,
In the afterglow, we learn to fly.

The Tapestry of Winter's Breath

Winter weaves her silver thread,
A tapestry where dreams are bred.
Frosty patterns on the window pane,
Nature's quilt, a soft refrain.

Whispers of snow in the quiet night,
Blanketing earth in purest white.
Each flake unique, a soaring song,
In winter's world, we all belong.

Branches adorned, a crystal lace,
Silent stillness in this sacred space.
Beneath the stars, the world holds its breath,
In the warmth of dreams, defying death.

Footsteps crunch on the frosty ground,
In the hush of night, there's beauty found.
The tapestry glimmers, a sight to behold,
In winter's embrace, stories unfold.

With every gust, a tale is spun,
Through the chill, life has just begun.
In this season, our hearts take flight,
Winter's breath whispers sweet goodnight.

Serene Nightfall

As the sun dips low, a calm descends,
The world slows down, as daylight ends.
Whispers of shadows embrace the land,
In serene nightfall, we take our stand.

Stars sprinkle silver on velvet skies,
Glimmers of hope in the dark arise.
Moonlight unfurls its gentle touch,
Cradling the night, it's never too much.

The soft hum of crickets fills the air,
Nature's lullaby, a tender prayer.
Each moment pauses, the heart beats slow,
In the tranquil dusk, the spirit will grow.

Dreams drift softly on the evening breeze,
Wrapping us in warmth, like the finest fleece.
Under the blanket of night's sweet song,
In serene nightfall, we all belong.

Hope sparkles bright in the quiet night,
As we surrender to soft twilight.
In the embrace of the stars above,
Serene nightfall whispers tales of love.

Glistening Shadows

In the quiet of the dusk, they dance,
Whispers on the wind, a fleeting chance.
Soft secrets linger in the air,
Glistening shadows, tender and rare.

Beneath the trees where silence thrived,
Silhouettes of dreams, alive, derived.
They flicker lightly as night descends,
Glistening shadows where hope transcends.

With every step, a story unfolds,
In the arms of darkness, their magic holds.
A world unseen by the passing eyes,
Glistening shadows under starlit skies.

For in these shades, the heart finds peace,
Moments of stillness, where sorrows cease.
A tranquil dance beneath the moon,
Glistening shadows hum a soft tune.

Each breath a prayer, each sigh a song,
In this embrace, where we belong.
Through the night, they softly flow,
Glistening shadows, in a gentle glow.

Moonlit Crystals

Underneath the silver beam,
Moonlit crystals shimmer and dream.
Reflections of a world anew,
Beauty captured in vibrant hue.

They twinkle like stars on gentle seas,
A dance of light in the evening breeze.
Every facet whispers a tale,
Moonlit crystals in the night prevail.

As darkness falls, they start to gleam,
A symphony of hope—a radiant theme.
In their glow, lost wonders roam,
Moonlit crystals, bringing us home.

Each drop of light a wish set free,
Echoes of laughter, soft as can be.
In the quiet, their magic sings,
Moonlit crystals, the joy life brings.

Together they weave a spell divine,
Glimmers of a world forever entwined.
Lost in the shimmer, we find our way,
Moonlit crystals guide our hearts to stay.

Translucent Pathways

Through the trees, an avenue shines,
Translucent pathways, soft, like lines.
Leading us on to realms unheard,
Whispers of nature in every word.

Beneath the canopy of stars so bright,
Guiding our fears into the light.
Each step reveals a story fair,
Translucent pathways, beyond compare.

In the stillness where shadows play,
Echoes of dreams will show the way.
Nature's canvas, vast and wide,
Translucent pathways as our guide.

They weave through time, a gentle flow,
Carving through hearts to make them glow.
A journey shared, a bond so strong,
Translucent pathways where we belong.

In every turn, a chance to find,
The beauty within, the ties that bind.
So let us wander, let us roam,
Translucent pathways lead us home.

Nebula of Light

In the cosmos where wonders spin,
A nebula of light where dreams begin.
Colors entwined in a cosmic dance,
A celestial embrace, a whispered chance.

Stars emerge from the vibrant hue,
Infection of beauty, vibrant and true.
Each flicker tells of ages past,
Nebula of light, a spell so vast.

With every breath, the universe sighs,
Galaxies twirling in endless skies.
A tapestry woven with cosmic art,
Nebula of light, igniting the heart.

Through space we travel, boundless and free,
In this expanse, we find our key.
An invitation to embrace the night,
Nebula of light, a soul's delight.

In silent awe, we gaze and dream,
Universe vast, an endless stream.
Unlocking mysteries that time ignites,
Nebula of light, our guiding sights.

A Dance of Luminescence

In night's embrace, the stars align,
A flicker of hope, a soft design.
They twirl and sway, in cosmic grace,
Whispers of light, in infinite space.

Dreams take flight on silver beams,
Carving paths through darkened dreams.
Every heartbeat, a gentle sigh,
As we dance beneath the sky.

The moonlight drapes, a silky veil,
Guiding us through the twilight trail.
With every step, a spark ignites,
Painting shadows with glowing sites.

Embrace the magic, let it flow,
In this waltz where all can glow.
Luminous hearts, intertwined,
In the soft night air, love defined.

Together we weave, a tapestry bright,
A dance of luminescence, pure delight.
In this fleeting moment, hearts collide,
As the cosmos watches, side by side.

The Glow Beneath

In the hush of dusk, secrets arise,
A tender glow beneath the skies.
Soft shadows play, as day departs,
Illuminating the hidden parts.

Beneath the surface, a gentle gleam,
Whispers of dreams in the night's stream.
Every moment, an ember lights,
Guiding lost souls to newfound heights.

Rustling leaves in a quiet dance,
Awakening hearts to life's sweet chance.
A spark of wonder in the air,
Holding answers to questions rare.

In darkened corners, truths are found,
The glow beneath, a vital sound.
It calls us forth to seek and see,
In every shadow, the light to be.

So let us wander, paths unknown,
Follow the glow that feels like home.
Together we'll step into the bright,
Unraveling dreams, igniting the night.

Sparkling Shadows

In twilight's hush, shadows arise,
Sparkling softly with glimmering sighs.
They weave a tale of love and fear,
Echoes whispering, drawing near.

Each flicker holds a memory dear,
A spark of laughter, a trace of tears.
They dance on walls, with gentle grace,
Carving memories in time's embrace.

With every heartbeat, shadows play,
A dance of light that fades away.
Painting the night with stories old,
In sparkling hues, their mysteries unfold.

What lies within those shadows deep?
A treasure trove for hearts to keep.
Connections made, with every glance,
In sparkling shadows, we take our chance.

So let us cherish these fleeting sights,
The magic found in silent nights.
For in the shadows, truth emerges,
A dance of light, as hope resurges.

Illusive Brilliance

Through corridors of light, we roam,
Chasing whispers that lead us home.
An illusive brilliance, shining bright,
Guiding our souls through the endless night.

Mirrors reflecting the dreams we chase,
A dance of shadows in an embrace.
Fleeting moments, glimmers we seek,
In every echo, the heart can speak.

As stars awaken with a silent call,
Each flicker reminds us, we rise or fall.
Illusions blend with reality's art,
Crafting a world where we all take part.

In dreams we wander, together we glide,
Exploring the realms where secrets abide.
An intricate tapestry, life intertwined,
With threads of brilliance, eternally aligned.

So here we stand, side by side,
In this dazzling dance where hopes abide.
For in the illusive depths we find,
A brilliance unbound, forever enshrined.

The Realm of Glassy Dreams

In the stillness of night, softly gleams,
Beneath the stars, where quiet beams.
Whispers of hope in a silken flow,
Fragile as dew, in the moon's soft glow.

Through borders unseen, into realms untold,
Echoes of wishes, in silence, unfold.
Mirrored reflections dance in the mist,
Caught in the fabric of dreams, we exist.

Each step is gentle, like snow on the ground,
In this realm of glass, where wonders abound.
Floating on currents of luminous light,
We drift through the shadows, embracing the night.

In this haven of peace, hearts intertwine,
Feeling the pulse of the celestial line.
Lost in enchantments, we wander and weave,
In the realm of glassy dreams, we believe.

Moments suspended, like breath in the air,
Here we find solace, stripped of all care.
Together we venture where dreams like to soar,
In this vibrant world, forever explore.

Unraveled Nightfall

As daylight fades into shadows dim,
The world transforms, as the light grows thin.
Threads of twilight weave a soft embrace,
Calling us softly to this sacred place.

Stars ignite softly, one after the other,
Each a reminder of a sleeping mother.
Night whispers secrets, rich and profound,
In the tapestry of silence, we are found.

Moonlight drapes gently, a silken sheet,
Where darkness and magic joyfully meet.
Shadows around us in tranquil delight,
Unraveled nightfall, a canvas of night.

The air holds a promise of dreams yet to chase,
As we weave our stories in the starlit space.
In every heartbeat, the night sings a hymn,
Drawing us closer, our spirits in swim.

Beneath the vast heavens, we find our way,
Guided by whispers that night sighed today.
With every step taken, we dance through the dark,
Unraveled nightfall, igniting our spark.

A Canvas of Frost

Morning light spills on a sparkling sheet,
Nature adorned, a whimsical treat.
Each crystal formed tells a story so bright,
In silence, it glimmers, a canvas of white.

Trees wear their coats of magical lace,
Delicate patterns, a frosty embrace.
Every breath whispers in chill of the dawn,
A symphony played as the world's gently drawn.

Footprints lay bare on this shimmering ground,
A moment captured, where beauty is found.
In the stillness, a soft lullaby hums,
Each stroke of frost tells of winter's sweet drums.

As daylight breaks, shadows softly retreat,
Nature's grand artwork, so tender, so sweet.
A canvas alive with the pulse of the cold,
Each frost-kissed whisper, a memory bold.

In the heart of the winter, life shines its truth,
Through frost and through chill, we embrace our youth.
In this masterpiece, pure and endlessly lost,
We find our reflections on a canvas of frost.

The Elegance of Darkness

Draped in a cloak of the deepest night,
Whispers of elegance take wing in flight.
Softly, the shadows begin to unfold,
A realm where the mysteries subtly are told.

In the depth of stillness, beauty does thrive,
A dance of the stars, where dreams come alive.
Every heartbeat syncs with the pulse of the void,
In the elegance of darkness, fears are destroyed.

Painted in secrets, the night sky gleams,
Floating on echoes of wistful dreams.
In shadowy corners, enchantments ignite,
Illuminating paths with the heart's quiet light.

Glimmers of hope pierce the veil of despair,
In the tranquil embrace, we find solace rare.
The elegance whispers, with every dark sigh,
Telling us stories that long to soar high.

In the swath of the night, our souls take their flight,
Embracing the chance to dance with the night.
In the elegance of darkness, we cherish the grace,
Finding our courage in this timeless place.

Radiant Illusions

In a world where shadows blend,
Colors dance and light won't bend.
Dreams take form, a vibrant hue,
Whispers of a life anew.

Mirrors show what hearts conceal,
Fragments of a grander reel.
With each glance, the truth does sway,
Guiding us along the way.

Fleeting moments, soft and bright,
Twinkling like the stars at night.
Every wish upon a star,
Brings our fantasies from far.

Through the mist of fading light,
Hope ignites the darkest night.
Radiant beams of joy arise,
Painting wonders in our skies.

In these visions, we find grace,
Lost in time, yet in this space.
Sweet illusions, ever near,
Capturing our every tear.

Celestial Echoes

Beneath a sky of endless blue,
Stars respond to dreams so true.
Whispers travel through the night,
Guiding souls with gentle light.

Galaxies in spiral dance,
Every star a chance, a chance.
In the void, a soft embrace,
Echoes fill the vastness' space.

Moments linger, hearts entwined,
Lost in thoughts we often find.
Celestial rhythms softly hum,
In the stillness, life will come.

Symphonies of night unfold,
Every story yet untold.
In the silence, beauty grows,
As the cosmic wind softly blows.

Upon horizons, dreams will soar,
Celestial echoes evermore.
With each heartbeat, love's refrain,
Links our spirits through the pain.

Midnight Reverie

In the hush of midnight glow,
Secrets in the breezes flow.
Dreams now take their careful flight,
In the shadow of the night.

Stars above begin to gleam,
Weaving paths within our dream.
In this quiet, thoughts can race,
Finding solace in this space.

Every whisper, soft and clear,
Brings the world a touch of cheer.
Moments linger, time stands still,
As the night unfolds its thrill.

Dancing shadows, silken thread,
Woven tales of words unsaid.
Floating on the midnight air,
Reveries both light and rare.

In these hours, hearts collide,
Bringing passion, deep inside.
Each soft echo builds anew,
In the moon's enchanting view.

Frosted Whispers

In the dawn of winter's breath,
Nature speaks of life and death.
Frosted whispers on the ground,
Softly sing, a crystal sound.

Branches glisten, laden low,
In the light, a graceful glow.
Every flake, a tale untold,
Woven finely, crisp and cold.

Through the stillness, secrets glide,
Beneath the snow, dreams abide.
In the quiet, hope reclaims,
All that stillness gently names.

Patterns form where bodies tread,
Soft impressions, lightly spread.
Nature's canvas, pure and bright,
Frosted dreams in morning light.

Beneath the cover, warmth will rise,
In the heart, the ember lies.
Frosted whispers, sweet and true,
Promise spring in skies of blue.

Night's Brilliant Cascade

Stars twinkle high with grace,
Moonlight dances on the lake.
Whispers of night softly trace,
A canvas where dreams awake.

Waves of silver gently glide,
Carrying secrets of the deep.
In this realm where hearts abide,
Lost in the magic, we leap.

Shadows stretch beneath the trees,
Nature breathes in tranquil song.
A breeze stirs the silent leaves,
Inviting us to dream along.

The night, a veil of pure delight,
Holds the warmth of all our fears.
In the glow of soft moonlight,
We find solace through the years.

Together in this sacred space,
Time stands still, a fleeting thread.
Each moment, a sweet embrace,
A tapestry of words unsaid.

Frosty Hues of Desire

In the garden, frost does cling,
Painting whispers on each bud.
Winter's touch, a silent sting,
Kisses bloom in frozen mud.

Crystalline dreams etched in air,
Shimmers of longing take flight.
Each glimmer, a breath of care,
A spark igniting the night.

Frigid breaths that softly sigh,
Embers hidden in the cold.
With each flicker, we defy,
The chill that keeps us controlled.

Through the gloom, a warmth we seek,
Passions buried in a frost.
While the world may seem so bleak,
In our hearts, we count the cost.

Beneath the white, a pulse beats near,
Each snowflake a promise bright.
In frost's embrace, we persevere,
Finding love within the night.

Shrouded in Brilliance

Behind the veil of twilight's glow,
A realm where secrets softly stir.
Glimmers of gold, a radiant show,
Illuminating thoughts that blur.

Veils of mist weave tales untold,
Where shadows play and whispers blend.
In this dance of blue and gold,
Hearts entwine, and spirits mend.

Each pulse of light breaks through the dark,
Casting flickers of hope so bright.
The heart awakens with a spark,
Chasing dreams into the night.

In spaces where silence prevails,
Secrets linger like soft sighs.
Every moment, a story trails,
Written in the starlit skies.

Brilliance shrouded, yet so near,
Whispers float upon the breeze.
In the quiet, we find no fear,
Together, our souls find ease.

The Fable of Ice and Light

In winter's grasp, a tale unfolds,
Of shimmering ice and radiant beams.
Beauty lies in the frost that holds,
A world reflecting our deepest dreams.

Icicles hang like crystal spears,
Glistening in the morning sun.
Each drop a promise, casting fears,
Sculpting hope for everyone.

Light dances on the frozen streams,
A symphony of colors bright.
In the quiet, life gently teems,
Awakening the perfect night.

Whispers of stories long forgot,
Echoes beneath the winter's chill.
In this realm where warmth is sought,
Shadows play with a loving thrill.

The fable we weave in the cold,
Of ice and light, of laughter and tears.
In each heartbeat, our truth is told,
A tapestry spun through the years.

Radiant Silence

In the hush of twilight's grace,
Stars awaken, take their place.
Whispers dance on breezy air,
Nature's beauty, pure and rare.

Moonlight kisses darkened trees,
Tranquil night, a gentle breeze.
Hearts alight with calm embrace,
Radiant silence finds its space.

Shadows stretch, the world at rest,
In stillness, we are truly blessed.
Time stands still, a sacred pause,
Silent wonders make us pause.

Voices fade, but dreams ignite,
Painting stories through the night.
In this realm of quiet dreams,
All is golden, or so it seems.

When dawn arrives, the silence breaks,
Another day, a chance to wake.
Yet in our hearts, the quiet stays,
Radiant silence guides our ways.

Frostbitten Fantasies

In the glimmer of winter's breath,
Whispers of dreams dance with death.
Frosted trees in quiet spell,
Echoes of stories only they tell.

Snowflakes twirl in gentle flight,
Each unique, a pure delight.
Cold embraces, crisp and clear,
Frostbitten fantasies appear.

In moonlight's glow, shadows play,
Chasing thoughts that drift away.
Frozen visions, secrets spun,
A world transformed, all is one.

Beneath the ice, life softly waits,
Nature's pause before the fates.
With every breath, a frosty sigh,
In fantasies, we learn to fly.

As dawn approaches, warmth will rise,
But for now, we close our eyes.
Holding tight to dreams so bright,
Frostbitten fantasies take flight.

The Frosted Lens

Through a lens of winter's hand,
We glimpse a softly frozen land.
Patterns form in crystal light,
Nature's art within our sight.

Footsteps crunch on powdered snow,
Each moment, time moves slow.
Behind the veil, a world of white,
Dreams unfold in pure delight.

In the stillness, silence reigns,
Every heartbeat, nature's chains.
Framed in frost, a perfect view,
The frosted lens reveals the true.

Clouds above in hues of gray,
Foreshadowing a brighter day.
Yet in the chill, we find our peace,
In frozen beauty, worries cease.

Through a lens, we see the whole,
Winter's touch, a quiet soul.
Capturing moments, fleeting fast,
The frosted lens, a spell that's cast.

Shards of Light

In the dawn where shadows play,
Morning breaks, a brand new day.
Shards of light kiss the cold ground,
A tapestry of colors found.

Hope awakens, whispers soft,
Carried high on breezes aloft.
Promises glimmer in the skies,
As the sun begins to rise.

Every ray, a tale to tell,
Breaking through the night's dark shell.
Reflecting life in every hue,
Shards of light bring warmth anew.

In the dance of day and night,
We find strength in every fight.
Hold on tight to dreams in sight,
For we are made of shards of light.

At dusk, the colors gently fade,
Yet in our hearts, the warmth is laid.
In every shadow, glimmers bright,
Forever bound by shards of light.

Stars in Glass

In a night of velvet dark,
Stars shimmer bright and far,
Captured in crystal frames,
Wishing on each twinkling spar.

Gazing through the polished pane,
Time whispers soft and sweet,
Memories of distant worlds,
In reflections, dreams meet.

Twinkling gems on blackened skies,
A canvas of endless grace,
Bottled wishes, hopes collide,
In this celestial space.

Holding light in fragile hands,
Moments forever freeze,
The universe paints its dance,
In glimmers, we find peace.

Dreamscapes of Luminescence

In shadows deep, a light appears,
Soft whispers guide the way,
Dreams unfold in colors bright,
Where night sings into day.

Glimmers dance on silken clouds,
A tapestry of night,
Each thread woven with magic,
Crafted from pure delight.

Floating high on beams of gold,
Moments drift and sway,
In a world where dreams take flight,
Every wish at play.

Echoes of the stars align,
Painting paths to roam,
In this dreamscape, hearts ignite,
Finding light, our home.

A Tinge of Frost

Morning whispers soft and light,
A blanket of crystal dew,
Nature dons her frosty veil,
As dawn breaks, fresh and new.

Each blade of grass, a diamond's spark,
In winter's gentle hold,
A shimmering tale of quiet grace,
In hues of blue and gold.

The world breathes in a silver hush,
Underneath the pale sun,
Frost-kissed dreams awaken still,
While winter's song is spun.

Traces of cold linger on air,
As shadows start to fade,
In the heart of this soft embrace,
The beauty of frost displayed.

The Glow of Quietude

In twilight's hush, a warmth unfolds,
The glow of soft repose,
A moment wrapped in serenity,
Where whispered stillness grows.

Candles flicker, shadows sway,
Illuminating the night,
In each quiet, gentle breath,
The world feels pure and right.

Beneath the stars, a tranquil heart,
Relaxes in their gaze,
The glow of quietude embraces,
In the night's gentle maze.

Time drifts slow, as dreams align,
In the tapestry of dark,
Peace ignites, a subtle blaze,
A calming, celestial spark.

Twilight's Embrace

The sun dips low, a golden thread,
Whispers of night weave softly instead.
Shadows stretch long, a gentle sigh,
As day concedes to the twilight sky.

Stars awaken, their twinkle bright,
Casting dreams on the canvas of night.
Moonlight spills like a silver stream,
Embracing all in a tranquil dream.

Crickets sing their evening song,
Nature hums, where hearts belong.
Cool breeze carries a sweet perfume,
Dancing softly in the evening gloom.

The world slows down, a tender grace,
In twilight's arms, we find our place.
Every heartbeat, a soothing balm,
In this moment, the night feels calm.

Silvery Serenade

Beneath the moon, a silver glow,
Rippling waters, a soft-flowing show.
Whispers carried by the night air,
Melodies linger, enchanting and rare.

The world transformed in shades of light,
Dance of shadows, a shimmering sight.
Stars compose their silent song,
Each note promising where dreams belong.

In the stillness, hearts align,
Rhythms echo, a sweet design.
Underneath the vast canvas spread,
Silvery dreams, where none would tread.

Time suspends in this gentle space,
Every moment a soft embrace.
The night whispers secrets untold,
In silvery hues, a magic bold.

The Chime of Stars

In the night sky, a chime rings clear,
Echoes of light, drawing us near.
Stars resonate with tales untold,
Whispers of ages, both bright and old.

As constellations weave their dance,
The universe sings, a timeless romance.
Galaxies swirl in a cosmic embrace,
A reminder of wonder in this vast space.

The chime of stars, a celestial train,
Guiding lost souls through joy and pain.
In their glow, hearts find their way,
A compass of dreams in the night's ballet.

Each twinkle a promise, a wish to hold,
Stories of stardust, in whispers foretold.
Through the dark, their brilliance will shine,
A tapestry woven, divine and benign.

Glacial Serenade

In frozen realms of ice and snow,
Whispers of winter in a gentle flow.
Glaciers glisten, a crystal sheen,
Nature's art in hues serene.

Frosted branches sway and bend,
Under the weight that winter sends.
Silent echoes in the chill of night,
In this stillness, everything feels right.

Snowflakes dance on a breath of air,
Each unique, a beauty rare.
A serenade of nature's grace,
In glacial zones, we find our place.

The cold caress, both firm and light,
Encases us in warmth despite.
In every layer, history told,
A timeless story, forever bold.

Melodies of Eternal Light

Whispers in the morning glow,
Awakening the world below.
Sunrise paints the sky so bright,
Dancing all with pure delight.

Songs of joy in softest breeze,
Floating gently through the trees.
Hopeful hearts in harmony,
Echoing eternity.

Stars that twinkle in the night,
Guide us with their gentle light.
Every note a sweet embrace,
Filling up this sacred space.

Radiant beams of love unfold,
Stories waiting to be told.
Moments cherished, fleeting flight,
Carried on the wings of light.

In this realm where dreams ignite,
Melodies of purest white.
Union of the soul's delight,
Blossoms in the warmest night.

Glacial Serenade

Whispers of the icy breeze,
Calm the heart, set it at ease.
Mountains high, their secrets keep,
In the silence, shadows sleep.

Blue and white in hues so bright,
Glistening under pale starlight.
Echoes of a cold embrace,
Nature's breath, a perfect grace.

Crystals form on branches bare,
As winter weaves its frosty care.
Melodies of frozen dreams,
Flowing through the tranquil streams.

Each flake falls, a unique song,
Tales of where the souls belong.
Softly hums the frozen land,
In the stillness, peace will stand.

Serenades that chill the air,
Wrap the world in pureness rare.
Harmony in frozen night,
Glacial beauty, pure delight.

Shimmering Shadows

Dancing in the evening glow,
Whispers of the night will flow.
Moonlight paints the world anew,
Shadows deep, a soft debut.

Glimmers of the stars above,
Shimmering with tales of love.
Every shadow tells a story,
Wrapped in silver, draped in glory.

Echoes of a distant song,
In the darkness, we belong.
Waves of twilight, soft and bright,
Embrace us in the mystic night.

Flickering light in soft refrain,
Gentle tides of sweetened pain.
Swaying leads to gentle dreams,
As starlit love silently gleams.

In the dance of shadowed grace,
Find the warmth of each embrace.
Whispered dreams in quiet flight,
Guide us through the endless night.

Celestial Reflections

Through the cosmos, stars align,
In the depths, their stories shine.
Mirrored worlds in peaceful dance,
Invite the heart to take a chance.

Galaxies of dreams unspooled,
In the silence, wisdom ruled.
Every spark, a soft embrace,
Echoes of a timeless grace.

Planets hum their ancient song,
Drawing us, where we belong.
Veils of dusk, the night unfolds,
In reflections pure as gold.

Universal tides will flow,
In our souls, we come to know.
Celestial paths beneath our feet,
Woven with a rhythm sweet.

In the cradle of the night,
Find the dawn's inviting light.
Every star, a thread connecting,
In the dark, our hearts are specting.

Veils of Enchantment

In moonlit gardens, shadows play,
Whispers of night, soft as a sway.
Petals tremble in a gentle breeze,
  Secrets linger among the trees.

Stars twinkle above in velvet skies,
Each glimmer tells of ancient ties.
Mysteries weave in the silken air,
Veils of enchantment, unaware.

A river flows with a silent hymn,
Reflecting dreams that never dim.
Crickets serenade the fading light,
Guiding the souls through the night.

Fingers of twilight brush the ground,
Lost in the magic that can be found.
Every sigh a soft, sweet embrace,
Within the night's eternal grace.

In the distance, a lone owl calls,
Echoing through twilight's gentle walls.
Veils of enchantment cloaked in hue,
Wrap the world in dreams anew.

Shards of the Cosmos

Under a dome of indigo light,
Fragments of stars dance in the night.
Galaxies whisper in ancient tongues,
Tales of the cosmic where time's unsung.

Each twinkle a spark, a story to tell,
Mysteries hidden in the celestial shell.
Light-years traverse through the vast unknown,
Inward, we gaze at the stars we've grown.

Nebulae twirl in a colorful spin,
Threads of creation where dreams begin.
Asteroids wander through silence profound,
Bearing secrets of worlds unbound.

Awake in the echoes of twilight's glow,
The dance of the heavens starts to flow.
Shards of the cosmos, bright and bold,
Unveiling stories that never grow old.

In whispers of gravity, fate intertwines,
With every heartbeat, a star aligns.
Celestial wonders, forever in flight,
Shards of the cosmos ignite the night.

Echoes of a Dimming Day

When the sun dips low in the sky's embrace,
Colors of dusk paint the world with grace.
Shadows lengthen, and whispers arise,
Echoes of a day meld with soft sighs.

Crimson and gold in a final dance,
Moments fleeting in this twilight chance.
As silence descends, the world holds its breath,
In the stillness lies a hint of death.

The horizon blushes, a soft farewell,
Stories untold in the twilight dwell.
Birds settle down, nestling in trees,
Nature hushes with the evening breeze.

A distant star claims its spot in the night,
Guiding the weary with its gentle light.
The moon rises high, bringing peace its way,
Echoes of a dimming day softly sway.

In dreams where the shadows and whispers meet,
Life dances slow to a heartbeat's beat.
As the world succumbs to night's gentle play,
Echoes linger from a fading day.

Stardust Whispers

In the quiet corners of the celestial sea,
Stardust whispers, inviting the free.
Thoughts like comets streak through the mind,
Dreams intertwined, a tapestry designed.

Moonbeams gather in soft, silver pools,
Lighting the paths of forgotten rules.
Each twinkle a promise of wishes made,
In the stardust, a magic cascade.

Ethereal breezes cradle the night,
Caressing the world with a gentle light.
In the heart of darkness, stars still gleam,
Bestowing hope within every dream.

Floating through space on a sigh's embrace,
Lost in the wonder of the vast, open space.
As the cosmos cradles souls at play,
Stardust whispers our fears away.

With every heartbeat, the universe spins,
In the dance of eternity, love begins.
Here among stardust, we find our way,
Whispers of beauty, come what may.

Twinkling Whispers

In the hush of night, stars gleam bright,
Whispers of dreams take gentle flight.
Moonlight dances on silver streams,
Each twinkle holds a thousand dreams.

Breezes carry soft tales untold,
Secrets of hearts, tender and bold.
Night's dark veil, a canvas wide,
Sheltering hopes that in darkness abide.

Silent wishes ride the air,
Every heartbeat, a muted prayer.
Among the shadows, shadows play,
In twilight's grace, night cradles day.

Stars waltz lightly in velvet skies,
Painting stories with gleaming ties.
Celestial whispers, soft and clear,
Embrace the soul, banish all fear.

With every twinkle, a world begins,
In the silence, the heart softly spins.
Night unfolds a gentle dream,
In twinkling whispers, we find our stream.

Spectral Glow

In the dim light, shadows play,
Colors shift, then fade away.
Whispers rise from time's deep well,
In spectral glow, their stories swell.

Veils of mist in the cool night air,
Guide the lost with gentle care.
Phantom lights dance on the ground,
In their embrace, lost souls are found.

Each flicker breathes a tale of old,
Mystic truths in hues so bold.
Glimmers hint at visions near,
Calling forth all that we hold dear.

Through the dark, a lantern's grace,
Shining bright in a timeless space.
In love's embrace, all shadows blend,
Spectral glow, where journeys end.

As the dawn starts to break the night,
Fading visions, a fleeting sight.
Yet in our hearts, the glow remains,
A tapestry of joy and pains.

Dancers on the Ice

Under the moon's soft, silver gaze,
Figures glide through a frozen haze.
Whirling lightly, laughter rings,
Dancers on the ice, with angel wings.

Crystal waters shimmer bright,
Waves of joy in the starry light.
Every movement, a tale retold,
In the heart where dreams unfold.

Twirls and spins, a graceful flight,
Embraced by the chill of night.
With every leap, a story unfolds,
In whispered breaths, the magic holds.

Warmth in the cold, souls intertwine,
In a rhythm where fates align.
With each glide, love's sweet refrain,
United footsteps, joy, and pain.

And when the sun begins to rise,
Painting gold across the skies,
The dancers rest, but not for long,
For ice holds them in an endless song.

Luminous Wanderlust

Beneath the stars, where dreams reside,
A path of light, a timeless guide.
With every step, the heart takes flight,
A luminous dance through the endless night.

Across the hills, to distant shores,
Each whisper calls, adventure soars.
In shadows stretched by moonlit beams,
Wanderers roam on woven dreams.

Fires crackle, tales unfold,
Of journeys brave and stories bold.
With glimmering eyes and spirits free,
The world awaits, a symphony.

Through valleys deep and mountains high,
Hearts entwined beneath the sky.
In every heartbeat, wanderlust glows,
A tale of wonder that never slows.

When morning dawns and night takes flight,
The journey breathes in endless light.
Always seeking, always true,
In luminous wanderlust, we renew.

Ethereal Tapestry

In the twilight's soft embrace,
Threads of silver start to trace,
Whispers glide through misty air,
Dreams entwined with cosmic flair.

Colors blend like water's hue,
Gossamer, the night's debut,
Stars awaken, brightly spun,
Woven tales in shadows run.

Moonlight dances on the seam,
Crafting visions from a dream,
Spectral patterns come alive,
In this realm where spirits thrive.

Luminous and ever bright,
Guiding hearts through endless night,
Each motif, a story told,
In the tapestry of old.

A tapestry of silent grace,
Echoes from a distant place,
Holding memories so dear,
In the weaving, all is clear.

Glimpses of Aurora

Beneath the canvas of the sky,
Colors mingle, dance, and fly,
Brushstrokes bright in colors bold,
Whispers of the night unfold.

Emerald greens and violet dreams,
Flicker softly, bursting beams,
Nature's palette, vast and wide,
In the dawn, we take our ride.

Celestial harmonies unfurl,
As day begins its gentle swirl,
Each glimpse a fleeting work of art,
Awakening the dreaming heart.

Radiant waves cascade and glide,
Across the heavens, worlds collide,
Moments captured, fleeting view,
Underneath the sky's embrace, so true.

In this spectacle, we gaze,
Lost in wonder, hearts ablaze,
As the sun and stars entwine,
In the dance of time divine.

The Sway of Night Gales

In the darkness, whispers play,
Stars above in soft ballet,
Wind's embrace begins to sway,
Carrying dreams away to stay.

Gentle sighs through trees resonate,
Transporting hearts to realms innate,
Nature's breath upon the hill,
Stirring souls with quiet thrill.

Shadows loom and dance about,
Filling silence with a shout,
In the night, the gales conspire,
Warming hearts and sparking fire.

Moonlit paths for wanderers bold,
Stories whispered, secrets told,
Each gust a lover's soft caress,
Embracing all with tenderness.

Through the dark, a melody,
Sways with time, so wild and free,
In the dance of night gales' tune,
Life's sweet song beneath the moon.

Starlit Mosaic

Fragments of light in skies so vast,
Scattered pieces of the past,
Crafting paths on midnight's floor,
A mosaic to explore.

Each twinkle holds a tale to weave,
Whispered dreams the night must give,
In the stillness, secrets shine,
Guiding souls through realms divine.

Patterns form as dark unfolds,
Threads of silver, stories bold,
In this cosmos, we are lost,
Finding beauty, no matter the cost.

Celestial art, a timeless sight,
Awakening the heart's delight,
As we gaze upon the twinkling sea,
Connected by our history.

In the starlit night's embrace,
Every moment leaves a trace,
A vibrant patchwork, woven bright,
In the depths of endless night.

Gossamer Lullabies

Softly weaving dreams so bright,
Stars are dancing, pure delight.
Moonlight spills on silken sheets,
As the world in slumber greets.

Gentle breezes hum a tune,
Crickets play beneath the moon.
Lullabies of nature's grace,
Wrap the night in a warm embrace.

Whispers flow through leafy trees,
Carried on the twilight breeze.
In this peace, our hearts will soar,
Gossamer dreams forevermore.

Sleepy shadows softly creep,
Guiding us to realms of sleep.
In the hush, the heartbeats slow,
While the night begins to glow.

With each sigh, the stars align,
In this dreamscape, we will shine.
Cradled in the arms of night,
Gossamer lullabies take flight.

Beneath the Silver Veil

A shimmer rests on quiet streams,
Where moonlight spills and softly gleams.
Beneath this veil, the world is hushed,
In gentle night, our hearts are flushed.

Whispers flutter, secrets shared,
In twilight's glow, we are ensnared.
Stars reveal what hearts conceal,
In silent vows beneath the wheel.

The shadows play on etched terrain,
Dancing lightly, casting grain.
Each heartbeat marks the time we steal,
Enfolded in this silver feel.

Night's caress, a tender weave,
Holding dreams that we believe.
Beneath the veil, we find our way,
In whispered promises, we stay.

As dawn approaches, colors blend,
Yet still in night, our spirits mend.
Beneath the silver's soft appeal,
We find our hope, our hearts reveal.

Whispers of Winter's Heart

Frosty breath upon the grass,
Winter whispers as shadows pass.
Softly blanketing the land,
In silence, nature takes a stand.

Branches heavy with sparkling snow,
Underneath, the pure winds blow.
Each flake dances a fragile art,
Telling tales of winter's heart.

Moonlit nights so crisp and clear,
Caroled joy that we hold dear.
In the hush, a world reborn,
With every breath, the dark's outworn.

Warmth of firesides, glowing bright,
Crackling logs, a peaceful light.
In this space, we feel the start,
Of hope renewed in winter's heart.

As the seasons shift and sway,
Let the whispers guide our way.
In the chill, love's ember burns,
Winter's heart, a lesson learns.

Twilight's Gleam

In twilight's bloom, the colors blend,
Hues of gold that softly send.
Kissed by dusk, the day must yield,
To night's embrace in magic field.

Golden rays begin to fade,
Casting shadows, softly laid.
In this space, our dreams take flight,
Chasing whispers of the night.

Stars awaken, one by one,
Filling skies when day is done.
Each glimmer tells a tale of old,
In twilight's gleam, the night unfolds.

Moonlight glimmers on the lake,
Mirrored secrets it will wake.
In this stillness, souls can roam,
Finding peace, we're never alone.

With every sigh, the world aligns,
In twilight's arms, our spirit shines.
As shadows dance, we let it beam,
And weave our hopes in twilight's gleam.

Enchanted Silence

In the hush of night I hear,
Whispers soft, crystal clear.
Stars are blinking, tempests fade,
In this stillness, dreams are made.

Moonlight dances on the ground,
Every shadow looks profound.
Time stands still, the world is lost,
In this calm, I feel the frost.

Gentle breezes brush my face,
Nature lingers, finds its place.
In the quiet, hope ignites,
Carried forth on peaceful nights.

Silence weaves a sacred thread,
Voices muted, fears are shed.
In its arms, my spirit soars,
Finding solace at its doors.

With each heartbeat, moments blend,
Enchanted stillness, love transcends.
Lost in wonder, here I stay,
Wrapped in silence, night and day.

Twilights and Ribbons

Twilight spills its colors bright,
Kissing shadows, chasing light.
Ribbons weave through branches fair,
Nature's canvas, beyond compare.

Golden hues and shades of blue,
Whispering tales, old and new.
In the fading light we find,
Magic draped in ties that bind.

Crickets sing their evening songs,
Harmony where each belongs.
As the night prepares to greet,
Every heartbeat, pulse discreet.

Starlit skies, a velvet dome,
In this moment, feel at home.
Threads of twilight softly sown,
A tapestry we've all known.

Ribbons curl, the world unwinds,
With each breath, a peace defines.
In the twilight's soft embrace,
We discover our true place.

Shining Whisper

In the dawn, a whisper glows,
Light that dances, gently flows.
Awakening the world anew,
In its beam, the heart breaks through.

Words unspoken drift on high,
Tales bestowed to only fly.
In the silence, promises bloom,
From the shadows, chase the gloom.

Each soft word holds stories deep,
In the quiet, secrets keep.
Through the air, they linger sweet,
Like a melody, soft and fleet.

Whispers travel, weaving dreams,
Carried forth on gentle streams.
In this radiance, hope ignites,
Horizons wrapped in golden sights.

With every breath, the moment grows,
In the shining, stillness flows.
Hold these whispers, quiet grace,
In their light, we find our place.

The Gaze of Gelid Dreams

In the night's cold, silver gleam,
Gelid visions, lost in dream.
Every star, a whispered thought,
In the stillness, warmth is sought.

Frozen echoes fill the air,
Secrets hidden, waiting there.
Through the frost, the heart beats slow,
Guided by the moonlit glow.

Chill of night embraces tight,
Glimmers sparkling, pure delight.
In this world of pale embrace,
Every shadow finds its place.

Gaze upon the dreams that freeze,
In their depths, a tranquil ease.
Feel the stillness wrap around,
In their silence, hope is found.

With each breath, the gelid chill,
Carves our wishes, bends our will.
In the night, where dreams take flight,
In the gaze of frost and light.

Frosted Euphony

Whispers of frost on silent ground,
A melody soft, a sweet sound.
Silver glimmers in the pale dawn,
Nature's hymn, where dreams are drawn.

Chill in the air, a crisp embrace,
Each step brings joy, a gentle pace.
Branches adorned with crystal lace,
In winter's arms, we find our place.

Echoes of laughter, pure delight,
Fireside stories through the night.
Stars twinkle in the velvet sky,
Serenading as time slips by.

Traces of hope in every breath,
Life's beauty, defying death.
In this frost, we find our tune,
Awakening dreams beneath the moon.

Harmony reigns in winter's chill,
As nature's heart begins to thrill.
Frosted euphony sings so sweet,
A moment's magic, pure and fleet.

Glittering Nightscapes

In twilight's grasp, the world transforms,
Jewel-toned skies, where starlight warms.
City lights flicker, a radiant glow,
Nightscapes unfold, a splendid show.

Whispers of dreams on the breeze,
Soft and fragrant, time to seize.
Moonlit paths invite to roam,
Under the heavens, far from home.

Reflections shimmer on calm waters,
In this silence, the heart falters.
Each twinkling star, a secret shared,
In nightscapes vast, we are ensnared.

Songs of the night dance through the air,
Every moment, a breath laid bare.
Time drifts slowly, lost in delight,
We find ourselves in the glittering night.

Delight in shadows, embrace the dark,
Each flicker ignites a hidden spark.
Nightscapes beckon, a tender call,
In their embrace, we lose it all.

The Sleep of Innocence

Soft lullabies hum through the night,
Cradled in dreams, held so tight.
Gentle breezes whisper low,
Innocence wrapped in twilight's glow.

Close your eyes to the world outside,
In this realm, no need to hide.
Calm as a river, pure and clear,
The sleep of innocence draws near.

Dancing shadows play on the wall,
In this stillness, hear the call.
Of tender winks and hopes held dear,
In dreams, we wander, free from fear.

Time flows softly, a gentle stream,
In the quiet, we softly dream.
Under the stars, we drift away,
Lost in the magic of the day.

Awake anew when dawn draws near,
With heart refreshed, free from fear.
The sleep of innocence, a soft refrain,
In its embrace, we live again.

Shards of Nocturnal Delight

Midnight's veil, where secrets meet,
Fragments of dreams at our feet.
The world transformed in shadows deep,
In shards of delight, our fantasies leap.

Glowing embers, the night ignites,
Flickering flames, enchanting sights.
Each whispering breeze tells a tale,
In this nocturnal dance, we prevail.

Moonlight strewn on cobblestone,
Every step brings us back home.
A cosmic riddle, stars sing bright,
Guiding our hearts through the night.

In laughter shared and glances quick,
Moments like shards, in memories stick.
Hold on to joy, let worries take flight,
In shadows we find our guiding light.

Embrace the stillness, let it unfold,
In the magic of night, we find the bold.
The shards of delight, they spark and gleam,
A truth we cherish, a shared dream.

Beacons of Cold

In the stillness of the night,
Stars twinkle with icy light,
Whispers carried on the breeze,
Nature's breath, a gentle tease.

Frosted fields and shadows dance,
Underneath the moon's romance,
Silver coats on trees so tall,
Embrace the beauty of it all.

Frigid air, a crisp delight,
Hearts warm in the starry sight,
Frozen lakes, reflections bright,
Guide us home through winter's night.

Candles flicker, spirits sing,
Chill of night, the joy it brings,
Beacons shining from afar,
Lighting paths, our guiding star.

In this world, where cold prevails,
Silent echoes weave their tales,
With every step, we feel the pull,
Of beacons bright and hearts so full.

Night's Dazzling Show

As dusk descends, the magic wakes,
A canvas drawn, the night remakes,
Stars ignite in a cosmic flow,
Nature's breath, a dazzling show.

Moonlight dances on the stream,
A silver thread, a whispered dream,
Crickets serenade the dark,
The night alive with brightened spark.

Clouds drift softly, shadows play,
Wonders woven in a ballet,
Each moment glows with mystic grace,
Embracing night's enchanting face.

Constellations weave their tales,
Guiding sailors, drifting sails,
Every twinkle, every glow,
In this night's alluring show.

Time stands still beneath the stars,
Peace descends, dissolving scars,
In the embrace of midnight's hue,
We find our dreams, a world anew.

The Splendor of Icy Whispers

Whispers ride the biting wind,
Secrets that the night rescinds,
Echoes soft as fallen snow,
Dancing lightly to and fro.

Frosted branches, stories shared,
With the moon, the night has dared,
Twinkling lights through winter's cloak,
In the silence, spirits woke.

Chilles shadows hover near,
In this quiet, crystal sphere,
Each heartbeat, crisp and clear,
Tunes of time we long to hear.

Glacial whispers cradle dreams,
Floating softly, silver beams,
Nature's breath, so cool and pure,
In this splendor, we endure.

Through the night, the wonders gleam,
In frozen radiance, a dream,
We find solace, hearts like feathers,
In the splendor of icy weathers.

Silvery Glimmer

Morning breaks with delicate light,
A silvery glimmer, pure and bright,
On the horizon, new hopes rise,
Painting dreams across the skies.

Gentle rays on glistening snow,
Whispers of a life we know,
Every shadow, every hue,
Carries tales of me and you.

With each step, a spark ignites,
Chasing shadows into sights,
Dreams reflected in a pool,
Nature's palette, calm and cool.

The world awakes from silent sleep,
In its grasp, the secrets keep,
A silvery glow that warms the heart,
In this moment, life's true art.

So let the light guide us through,
To newer days, to skies so blue,
In every glimmer, we shall see,
The beauty of what it means to be.

The Frosted Pavilion

In the glen where silence hums,
Snowflakes dance, the soft wind drums.
Crystal whispers in the light,
Embers fade into the night.

Beneath the beams of silver glow,
Time suspends in the fading fro.
Branches heavy with purest white,
Nature's quilt, a stunning sight.

Candle flames flicker, dreams ignite,
Every shadow, a tale to write.
The air, crisp with evening's breath,
Holds the secrets of life and death.

In this space where beauty weaves,
Hope and magic, the heart believes.
With each step, the world stills near,
In this pavilion, there's no fear.

As the dusk enfolds the scene,
Beneath the stars, a world serene.
We linger here, souls intertwined,
In the frost, our hearts aligned.

Secrets of the Night Sky

Whispers twirl on the moonlit breeze,
Stars above, like ancient keys.
Each constellational dance reveals,
Mysteries that the night conceals.

Pines stand tall, guardians of time,
Holding secrets in silent rhyme.
Voices echo through shadowed woods,
Carrying tales of hidden goods.

Galaxies spin in the velvet dark,
Flickering softly, each a spark.
Worlds colliding in timeless play,
Guiding dreams along the way.

With each gaze, our spirits soar,
Finding solace as we explore.
A canvas stretched across the dome,
Calling us, the stars our home.

Yet, in this realm, we stand alone,
With desires like seeds to sow.
Every twinkle offers a chance,
To meet the night in a cosmic dance.

Chasing Icicle Reflections

Icicles glisten, a winter's grace,
Mirrored shards in a frozen space.
Each drop captures a fleeting scene,
Reflecting wonders, so pure, so keen.

In puddles formed by melting light,
Images blur, twinkle bright.
With every shard, a story sways,
In the sun's warm, joyous rays.

Footprints trail on the snow-kissed ground,
Hearts echo in the silence found.
Nature's canvas, painted anew,
Framed in ice, embellished with blue.

Chasing moments, we gather near,
Holding dreams, casting out fear.
With each reflection, we unveil,
The beauty in life's shifting trail.

As shadows stretch and evening looms,
In this dance, our spirit blooms.
Icicles sparkle, a fleeting phase,
Our laughter echoes through the haze.

Luminescent Murmurs

In twilight's cradle, whispers sigh,
Softly glowing, like stars on high.
Each murmur holds a tale untold,
Within its warmth, the heart feels bold.

Sparrows flit in the amber light,
Flashing shadows, taking flight.
Voices blend in the gentle stream,
Flowing freely, like a dream.

Golden hues spill on the ground,
Stirring memories, lost but found.
Every step, a newly spun thread,
Weaving stories, where none are read.

The world hums with a tender glow,
Luminescent paths that gently flow.
In silence, secrets come alive,
In these murmurs, our spirits thrive.

With dusk enfolding our restless hearts,
We dance where the magic starts.
Embracing each moment, pure and bright,
In the glow of the gentle night.

Frosted Dreams

In a quiet dawn, the world is white,
Whispers of winter, soft and light.
Trees wear blankets of shimmering frost,
Each breath a cloud, the warmth we lost.

Footprints trudge on a path so deep,
Secrets of snow, the silence keeps.
Dreams like snowflakes, unique and rare,
Drifting softly through crisp, cold air.

Beneath the stars, the night unfolds,
Stories of chill, in silence told.
Lulled by the glow of a lantern's light,
Chasing the shadows that dance in the night.

As daylight breaks, the frost will fade,
Yet in our hearts, memories made.
Frosted dreams linger, never far,
Guiding us gently, like a bright star.

So let us weave, with threads of white,
A tapestry made of pure delight.
In winter's grasp, we find our peace,
Frosted dreams, may they never cease.

A Dance of Ice

Under the moon, the glaciers sway,
A dance of ice on a winter's day.
Each twirl and glide, a story spun,
Of frozen nights and the morning sun.

Snowflakes flutter like dancers bright,
Whirling and twirling in soft moonlight.
The rhythm of cold, a time-honored song,
Where whispers of winter, sweetly prolong.

With every step, the world holds its breath,
A ballet of nature, a graceful death.
The stillness enchants, a spellbound trance,
In this moment, our hearts find their dance.

Frosted figures move in a line,
Choreographed by the hand of time.
As dawn approaches, the curtain falls,
Yet echoes of beauty, forever calls.

In the glow of the day, the ice will wane,
But the memory lingers, the joy, the pain.
A dance of ice, etched in the mind,
In winter's embrace, true magic we find.

Glistening Illusions

Upon the lake, a mirror spreads,
Reflecting dreams, where silence treads.
Glistening illusions in morning's light,
A world transformed, a breathtaking sight.

The essence of chill hangs in the air,
A magical pause, so wonderfully rare.
Through branches bare, the sunlight beams,
Painting our hearts with radiant dreams.

Frosted jewels, on each blade of grass,
Moments of wonder, alas, they pass.
Nature's canvas, an art sublime,
Captured in crystal, suspended in time.

When shadows deepen and twilight glows,
The spark of enchantment quietly sows.
In every glimmer, the stories weave,
Of hopes and wishes we dare to believe.

Oh, glistening illusions, fleeting and bright,
You dance in our visions, a soft delight.
As twilight descends, we hold on tight,
To the magic of moments that ignite the night.

Nightfall's Radiance

As daylight wanes, the world transforms,
Nightfall's radiance in silver forms.
Stars like lanterns in the dusky sky,
Each twinkle a whisper, a lullaby.

The moon ascends, a regal sight,
Bathing the earth in soft, gentle light.
Mysteries stir in the cloak of dark,
In the silence, the night leaves a mark.

Winds dance slowly with a wistful sigh,
Secrets to share with the passing sky.
Shadows stretch where the dreams can roam,
Nightfall's embrace feels like coming home.

In the stillness, our spirits soar,
Lost in the magic, forevermore.
The glow of night, our hearts will trace,
In the quiet, we find our place.

As dawn approaches, the dream will wane,
Yet nightfall's radiance will not be in vain.
A tapestry woven with threads of light,
In every heart, a piece of the night.

Silver-touched Reveries

In whispers soft, the night descends,
With silver beams that twilight sends.
Across the fields, dreams gently sway,
In quietude, they dance and play.

The moonlight bathes each leaf and stone,
In shimmering hues, the world is shown.
With each breath, a story unfolds,
Of ancient tales and secrets told.

Stars twinkle bright, a brilliant chart,
Mapping the paths of the wandering heart.
In silver-touched reveries we dwell,
Our spirits soar, our worries quell.

As night bequeaths its tender grace,
We find ourselves in a timeless space.
With hope ignited, we yearn to dream,
In silver whispers, all is as it seems.

So close your eyes and take a flight,
Through silver-touched realms of night.
Where every moment paints the skies,
And dreams awaken, hearts arise.

Veiled Wonders

In shadows deep where secrets lie,
Veiled wonders wait, yet none know why.
A tapestry of dusk and dawn,
In every stitch, a magic drawn.

Whispers rustle through the trees,
Carried softly on the breeze.
Nature cradles hushed delights,
In realms of dark, in starlit nights.

Misty veils and hidden trails,
Where silence breathes and wonder hails.
The unseen pulses with a life,
In veiled mysteries, peace and strife.

Footsteps echo on the ground,
In sacredness, the world is found.
Every glance, a new disguise,
In veils of wonder, life belies.

So linger here, let intuition steer,
Through veiled wonders, far and near.
In the heart's embrace, we find our way,
To hidden treasures, come what may.

A Mirthful Chill

A mirthful chill creeps in at dusk,
The air a dance, the leaves a husk.
Laughter rings through twilight's breath,
In playful tones, we banish death.

The moonlight drapes on frosty ground,
In silver laughter, joy is found.
With every shiver, a tale is spun,
A mirthful chill, and we are one.

Hot cocoa warms our tired hands,
As winter speaks in hushed commands.
Together, we weave a tapestry,
Of joy and warmth, a jubilee.

Sparkling stars like candles bright,
Illuminate our shared delight.
In the chill, our hearts ignite,
With mirthful echoes, pure and bright.

So let the cold embrace our cheer,
Each breath we take, we hold it dear.
In every laugh, in every thrill,
We find our joy in a mirthful chill.

Beneath the Glittering Veil

Beneath the glittering veil at night,
Stars breathe secrets, bold and bright.
Each twinkling light, a story shared,
In celestial tales, we are ensnared.

The sky unfolds its velvet cloak,
Where dreams are whispered, hopes awoke.
In moments pure and thoughts serene,
Beneath the veil, life feels like a dream.

With every heartbeat, wonders grow,
As cosmic winds begin to flow.
The universe sings, a timeless song,
Where all belong, where all are strong.

Shimmering dust in silence glows,
In hidden paths the starlight knows.
A dance of fate, a chance to thrill,
In secrets kept beneath the still.

So lift your gaze to the skies above,
And feel the pull of a heart in love.
Beneath the glittering veil we find,
The essence of hope, entwined and blind.

Frost-kissed Horizons

Across the meadow, shadows play,
Frost-kissed blooms greet the day.
Sunlight glimmers, a gentle kiss,
Nature awakens, a moment of bliss.

Chill in the air, a soft embrace,
Whispers of winter in quiet space.
Footprints in snow tell tales of old,
Silent secrets in silence unfold.

Clouds drift slowly, a canvas bright,
Morning's glow, a pure delight.
Mountains stand tall, proud and grand,
Guardians watching this sacred land.

As twilight falls, the stars ignite,
Frost-kissed horizons, a breathtaking sight.
The moon lends magic, shadows entwine,
In nature's cradle, our spirits align.

With every breath, the chill retreats,
Life's symphony in quiet beats.
Frost-kissed whispers echo near,
A melody woven through each year.

The Whisper of Jewel-toned Hearts

In twilight's glow, we softly weave,
Whispers of dreams, we dare to believe.
Jewel-toned colors dance in the night,
Hearts entwined, a radiant sight.

Amidst the silence, a gentle sigh,
Stars above twinkle, one by one, they fly.
Each heartbeat echoes a tale untold,
In the warmth of love, we break the cold.

Petals unfurl in shades so bright,
The whisper of souls takes joyful flight.
In this moment, time stands still,
Jewel-toned hearts, a bond to fulfill.

Laughter rings out, like bells so clear,
Soft melodies linger, drawing us near.
Together we stand, hand in hand,
Anchored in love, a timeless strand.

As dawn awakens, the colors blend,
The whisper of hearts, on which we depend.
Through storms and sun, we'll never part,
Forever united, jewel-toned hearts.

Woven in Light

Threads of gold in the morning sun,
Woven in light, our stories run.
Each moment captured, a fleeting spark,
Illumined paths where dreams can embark.

In the fabric of life, colors entwine,
Patterns of joy, in every design.
Whispers of hope in every seam,
Weaving together our shared dream.

Dances of shadows, playful and free,
Illuminated visions for you and me.
Together we shine, a brilliant array,
Gifted by light, we find our way.

As twilight descends, the threads remain,
Woven in light, through joy and pain.
In every heartbeat, in laughter and tears,
We stitch our stories across the years.

The tapestry glows under the stars,
A symphony born from light's sweet scars.
In the weave of existence, we find our place,
Woven in light, an eternal embrace.

Ethereal Melodies

In twilight's hush, melodies soar,
Ethereal echoes that beckon for more.
Whispers of winds in harmony blend,
Notes like feathers, around me they send.

Moonlit serenades fill the air,
Dancing lightly without a care.
Stars shimmer softly, a cosmic refrain,
In this symphony, there's no pain.

Glimmers of laughter, the heart's delight,
Ethereal harmonies breaking the night.
The universe sways, in rhythm so pure,
With every heartbeat, our spirits endure.

As dawn unfolds, the music may wane,
Yet echoes linger, like soft summer rain.
We'll carry the song, in our hearts it will stay,
Ethereal melodies, lighting our way.

Together we'll journey, through shadows and light,
In the dance of existence, with futures so bright.
A tapestry woven, each note brings us near,
Ethereal melodies, forever we'll hear.

Luminous Twilight

The sun dips low behind the hills,
A canvas kissed with golden thrills.
Shadows stretch and gently play,
As night embraces the end of day.

Stars awaken in a velvet sky,
Whispers of the night draw nigh.
A breeze carries tales of old,
In twilight's glow, the secrets unfold.

Colors blend in soft embrace,
Nature's beauty finds its place.
The world turns quiet, still, and bright,
In the soft warmth of fading light.

Dreams begin to dance and sway,
Underneath the moon's gentle ray.
Each moment holds a hidden spark,
A promise lingered in the dark.

As darkness drapes, the stars ignite,
A symphony of shimmering light.
In luminous twilight's gentle weave,
We find the magic we believe.

Shards of Dusk

When day decays to dusk's embrace,
Time reveals its hidden face.
Fragments of the day are cast,
In shimmering shades and hues amassed.

The chirping crickets serenade,
With melodies that quickly fade.
Each shard of light a fleeting dream,
Dancing softly in twilight's beam.

Bare branches stretch against the sky,
In silhouettes, they rise up high.
The air is thick with whispered sighs,
As soft as laughter, light as lies.

In shadows deep, the colors blend,
Night and day begin to mend.
A tapestry of stars appears,
To cloak the world in cosmic gears.

From dusk's embrace, new dreams arise,
With glimmers caught in twilight's sighs.
In every moment, there lies trust,
In shards of dusk, all things adjust.

Ethereal Dreams

In the realm where shadows play,
Ethereal dreams begin to sway.
Whispers linger in the air,
Soft as petals, light as prayer.

Moonlit rivers gently flow,
Carrying secrets we don't know.
In every ripple, fantasies glide,
In the stillness, we confide.

The stars above like fireflies dance,
Inviting hearts to take a chance.
In the darkness, visions gleam,
A world awakened from a dream.

Mysterious paths entwine and weave,
In the fabric of night, we believe.
With each breath, the magic persists,
In ethereal dreams, we find bliss.

So close your eyes and drift away,
To the land where wishes play.
With tender hope and hearts that soar,
Ethereal dreams will open doors.

Glimmers in the Darkness

In shadows deep where silence reigns,
Hope flickers softly, breaking chains.
Glimmers of light, a guiding spark,
Illuminate the paths through dark.

Stars awaken, a distant choir,
Their shimmering notes lift us higher.
Each twinkle tells a story bold,
Of dreams in darkness waiting to unfold.

The night holds secrets, vast and wide,
In stillness, our fears we can't hide.
Yet glimmers welcome us to see,
The beauty found in mystery.

With every breath, the shadows sway,
Emotions rise, then drift away.
A dance of hope upon the ground,
In glimmers bright, our peace is found.

So seek the light amidst the night,
In every challenge, find the bright.
For in the dark, new chances start,
With glimmers guiding the hopeful heart.

A Night of Crystal Petals

Beneath the moon's soft glow, we tread,
Whispers in the night, where dreams are fed.
Petals fall like secrets shared,
In gardens where our hearts are bared.

Silver dew on blades that shine,
We dance through shadows, entwined in time.
A melody, so sweet and rare,
In this enchanted, fragrant air.

Stars wink above in cosmic play,
Guiding us gently on our way.
Footprints of starlight 'neath our feet,
A race of hearts, a rhythm sweet.

The echoes of laughter swirl and spin,
As night's embrace draws us further in.
In crystal dreams where silence reigns,
Love blooms softly like gentle rains.

Each fleeting moment, tender, bright,
A tapestry woven in the night.
With crystal petals all around,
In this sanctuary, joy is found.

Glazed Amidst the Stars

In the velvet sky, we find our place,
Each twinkling light, a familiar face.
Galaxies swirl in a cosmic dance,
Encircling us in a timeless trance.

The night air shimmers, cool and sweet,
As stardust whispers beneath our feet.
Amidst the chaos, calm resides,
With every breath, the cosmos glides.

Glazed in moonlight, we stand amazed,
Lost in the beauty, utterly dazed.
The world suspends in a fragile sigh,
Connected forever, you and I.

Each constellation tells a tale,
Of hope and longing in every trail.
In colors deep, the heavens call,
Underneath this vast, starry hall.

As dawn approaches with softest hue,
We'll carry the night within our view.
Glazed amidst the stars we roam,
Together, forever, we make our home.

Shivering Exhalations

Underneath a silvered sky,
Breath of winter whispers by.
Shivering trees in quiet mourn,
As night's chill weaves tales, forlorn.

Frosted air, a crystal song,
Echoes where our souls belong.
In the shadows, stories spin,
Of lost dreams and where we've been.

Exhalations dance on breath,
In this moment, we embrace death.
A flicker of warmth in the cold,
Tales of the brave yet oft retold.

Every heartbeat, a promise made,
In glimmering frost, life's sweet cascade.
Shivering silence, hearts laid bare,
In the winter's breath, love dares to share.

We walk this path, hand in hand,
Amidst the beauty of frozen land.
Shivering exhalations entwined,
Within this chill, we find our kind.

Chilled Echoes of Wonder

With whispered winds, the night unfolds,
Chilled echoes carry stories untold.
Amongst the shadows, secrets creep,
Where echoes of wonder silently seep.

Through the twilight, wonders gleam,
Fragments of a forgotten dream.
Stars shiver gently in their flight,
Painting the canvas of the night.

In this world of hushed delight,
We chase the echoes, hearts ignited.
Each sigh of wind, a soft embrace,
In the chill, we find our place.

The moon, a guardian overhead,
Guiding paths where spirits tread.
In every shimmer, a tale to weave,
Of moments cherished and love conceived.

Amongst the chilled echoes we roam,
In the arms of wonder, we find home.
Together in the night, forever bound,
Where magic lingers all around.

The Weight of Starlight

In the quiet night air, they gleam,
Whispers of wishes, a distant dream.
Each twinkle tells tales, soft and bright,
Carrying hopes on wings of light.

The sky, a blanket, woven with care,
Cradling secrets, floating in air.
Bringing solace to hearts that yearn,
In every shimmer, a lesson to learn.

Through the darkness, they guide the way,
Casting shadows where children play.
With every glance, a spark ignites,
Awakening love in endless nights.

Yet heavy they are, those bright little specs,
Full of dreams and the silent wrecks.
Each flaring pulse a precious weight,
Borne by souls that dance with fate.

So hold them close, those gems above,
In every heartbeat, a tale of love.
For in their glow, we find our light,
The weight of starlight, shining bright.

Cold Dances and Warm Dreams

With frosty breath, the night begins,
Crystals forming, nature spins.
Each flake a story, crisp and pure,
In the cold embrace, hearts endure.

Beneath the moon, shadows glide,
Silent whispers, where dreams reside.
Footprints vanish as they twirl,
In this dance, the night unfurls.

Warmth lies in the dreams we chase,
Embers glowing in a sacred space.
Fires burning, spirits high,
In the stillness, let time fly.

The chill may bite, but love ignites,
In the cold dances of starry nights.
Holding tight to hopes and schemes,
Through icy winds, we weave our dreams.

So let us spin in this frosty tune,
Beneath the watchful, pale moon.
For every chill, a warmth survives,
In cold dances, our passion thrives.

Twilight Adorned

The day takes flight, the twilight calls,
As shadows stretch on ancient walls.
Gold fades gentle into deep blue,
While soft sighs brush the earth anew.

Stars awaken, in vibrant swirl,
Painting dreams in a dusky pearl.
The dusk, a canvas, rich and wide,
Where the heart's secrets often hide.

In this hour, we find our peace,
As day's chaos begins to cease.
The whispers of night, an eerie song,
Embracing all that feels so wrong.

With twilight's grace, we dance and sway,
In the warmth of dusk, we let the day.
Adorned in whispers, cloaked in chance,
In twilight's embrace, we take our stance.

So linger here, as night unfolds,
Beneath the stars, our story told.
In every hue, a memory born,
In twilight adorned, a new dawn is sworn.

The Shimmering Threshold

At the edge of dreams, the threshold waits,
Where magic dances and time creates.
Beyond the veil, the past aligns,
In shimmering light, the future shines.

Each step whispers, urging us near,
To leap beyond what we hold dear.
With every glance, a door swings wide,
Inviting souls to the other side.

The air is thick with promise bright,
Carrying dreams, igniting light.
Beyond the threshold, hope takes flight,
In that gleam, the dark turns bright.

With hearts unleashed, we cross the line,
Into the realm where stars entwine.
The shimmering path, both wild and free,
Opens eyes to what can be.

So let us walk where shadows fade,
Embracing all the choices made.
For in this place, we find our worth,
The shimmering threshold, rebirth.

Milton Keynes UK
Ingram Content Group UK Ltd.
UKHW010231111224
452348UK00011B/663